DECADES

The FIFTIES

Tom Stacy

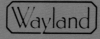

DECADES

The Fifties
The Sixties
The Seventies
The Eighties

First published in 1989 by
Wayland (Publishers) Ltd
61 Western Road, Hove
East Sussex BN3 1JD, England

Edited by Roger Coote
Designed by Helen White
Series Consultant: Stuart Laing
Dean of Cultural and Community Studies
University of Sussex

British Library Cataloguing in Publication Data

Stacy, Tom
The fifties
1. Great Britain, Young persons.
Social life, 1945-
I. Title   II. Series
941,085'088055

ISBN 1 85210 722 7

Typeset by Direct Image Photosetting Ltd
Hove, East Sussex, England
Printed in Italy by G. Canale and C.S.p.A., Turin
Bound in Belgium by Casterman S.A.

ROTHERHAM PUBLIC LIBRARIES

This book must be returned by the date specified at the time of
issue as the Date Due for Return.
The loan may be extended (personally, by post or telephone) for
a further period, if the book is not required by another reader,
by quoting the above number   **LM1 (C)**

Contents

Introduction

In 1950 the world was recovering from the devastation of the Second World War, which had ended five years earlier. The USA had emerged from the war as the undisputed 'superpower', but much of Europe lay in ruins. Defeated Germany was divided in two and, until 1952, occupied by the Allies. The Russians had lowered an 'iron curtain' across the continent, dividing East from West. In Asia, Japan (Germany's wartime ally) was rebuilding its shattered cities and factories. India had been an independent republic for just three years, while most of Africa was still ruled by the colonial powers. including Britain.

Above Dining out fifties-style. A couple on a date listen to a swing band while they eat.

The fifties was a time of great political tension and change. The peace that followed the war did not last long: the Korean War broke out in 1950. In 1952 the USA exploded the first hydrogen bomb at Eniwetok Atoll in the Pacific, followed a year later by Russia; the nuclear arsenals of East and West grew throughout the decade. In Britain, the Campaign for Nuclear Disarmament (CND) was founded in 1958 to press for the abolition of nuclear weapons. Independence movements came to the fore in Asia and Africa. In Europe the European Economic Community (EEC) was founded in 1957.

To grow up in Europe in the 1950s was to move from austerity, shortages and rationing to a new era of material affluence. The USA, meanwhile, was already the wealthiest nation on Earth, and the American way of life was envied throughout the Western world.

To be young in 1950 was to be young in a world where 'youth culture' hardly existed.

Young people were expected to conform, and to live and behave according to the values dictated by their elders. Most of them did so, although there was to be a growing spirit of rebellion and a new assertiveness of young ideas and styles.

During the fifties living standards rose steadily. Unemployment was low. People longed for a brighter, more lively world after the war and its aftermath, and gradually things began to happen. And it was the young who led the way. Young people were an increasingly important market for clothes and other goods. They developed their own tastes in music and fashion. They began to express their own opinions more forcibly. The term 'teenager' became familiar on both sides of the Atlantic.

Below London in the early fifties was slowly recovering from the effects of wartime bombing. Large areas of the city still looked like this. The Barbican development later rose from these ruins.

Above Americans enjoy a beach barbecue. Wartime shortages had little effect on life in the USA and in the fifties people's standard of living rose rapidly. The American way of life was envied and emulated.

In the space of ten years, a far-reaching social revolution had got under way. Its roots lay in the disruption of war, but its driving force came from the economic growth and technological advances of the West. The changes that took place in the 1950s were perhaps more noticeable than those of any succeeding decade. Their effects were felt everywhere — in the USA and Canada, in Britain, in Europe, in Australia and New Zealand, in Africa and Asia.

By 1960 the British Empire had become a new, more loosely knit 'family of nations' — the Commonwealth. The space age had begun with the launch of the world's first space satellite in 1957. There were nuclear-powered submarines beneath the seas and

nuclear power stations generating electricity on land. Television had become the centre of home entertainment and information, ousting the movies and newspapers. People were eager to buy the growing range of consumer and luxury goods — radios, televisions, washing machines, refrigerators, gadgets of every kind. The car dominated urban life in the United States, and was beginning to do the same in Europe. *All Shook Up* was a pop hit of the decade, and its title seems to symbolize what had happened to the world. The age of austerity had made way for the affluent society.

Above A fifties advertisement for vacuum cleaners and washing machines. The manufacturers appealed directly to women in the home, promising to abolish household drudgery for ever, the old-fashioned 'washday' in particular.

Above High fashion for the well-to-do. French couturier Pierre Balmain shows off a reversible evening cloak, 1950.

During the long war years of the forties, people had been starved of fashion. As peacetime production gradually got back to normal, a generation of young men and women looked eagerly to fashion designers for a new lead. Unless you were rich, there was disappointingly little to be excited about at first. 'High fashion' remained dominated by the expensive fashion houses — such as Norman Hartnell and Hardy Amies in London, Christian Dior and Pierre Balmain in Paris. Their original *haute couture* designs were too expensive for most shoppers, but they were copied in cheaper materials by the chain stores.

Above An advertiser's version of what well-dressed fifties children should wear. Parents found the choice of materials and styles widening, though children's fashions were less commercialized than they are today.

Below The clean-cut college look of fifties US fashion: for boys, short hair, shiny shoes, patterned ties and sweaters; for girls, short wavy hair, bright shiny lips, tight waists and accentuated busts.

Children in the 1950s looked very different from the way they do today. Boys wore short trousers, at least until they were 12 or so. Jeans were seldom seen outside the USA, where they were very much 'men-only'.

For a boy, his first pair of long trousers was a symbol of manhood. Young girls seldom wore trousers; their mothers dressed them in cotton dresses, or skirts, blouses and cardigans.

Teenagers tried to develop their own styles within the limited, but expanding, range of clothing available. There was an urge to show off and experiment. But very few designers were making clothing for the youth market; only in the USA were stores beginning to open 'young style' departments. British youngsters had to wait for new designers such as Mary Quant, who opened her first shop in London in 1955, for a fashion look that was bright, different and affordable.

Fashion for girls

A tomboy might rush around in long pants or jeans with the bottoms rolled up, but the average American teenage girl was more likely to go out for a date wearing a circular full skirt over lots of stiffened petticoats, short 'bobby socks' and flat shoes. Stiletto heels came a little later. Eventually, fashion designers and manufacturers realized a startling fact: two-thirds of the female population of the USA was under 30. There was a huge market waiting to be satisfied.

Films had a big influence on what young girls wore. Those with busts shocked their friends by squeezing into tight sweaters, just like film stars Jane Russell and Jayne

Above A fifties couple jiving. Dancing swirls out the bell-like skirt of the girl's typical check print dress. The casual look of her partner characterizes the leisure menswear of the period.

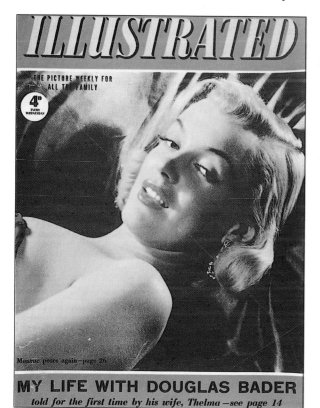

Above Fifties cover girl supreme: Marilyn Monroe. This cover photo from a July 1956 *Illustrated* magazine accentuates her 'sex-symbol' role and illustrates too the ideal look to which readers might aspire.

Mansfield. Another star, Marilyn Monroe, became the international pin up of the decade, her face and figure displayed everywhere. Sales of padded bras soared. The French coined the descriptive term: *le busty-look américain*.

The typical fifties look was tight-waisted, the swinging skirt worn with a belt and a shirt-style blouse. Wide skirts were fine for jiving — the favourite teenage dance of the time. Girls' hairstyles were generally soft curled. The pony tail was a popular hair fashion; another was the alice band. Towards the end of the fifties puffed-up, back-combed 'beehive' styles became fashionable.

New materials

The real revolution in fashion lay not so much in the look as in the materials. Science had come into the textile mill. Synthetic materials such as Orlon, Acrilan, Dacron and Poplin — developed following the breakthrough invention of nylon in the 1930s — were taking over from traditional wool and cotton. They were cheaper and they could be dyed in many colours. Many were 'drip dry', making washday less of a chore. The new materials were especially popular for underwear and men's shirts. Girls wore nylon stockings which were becoming cheaper and less liable to 'ladder' or run. Tights did not become popular until the sixties.

Above Young sharp dressers in the London of 1955. Elements of Teddy boy style are worn by the cigarette-smoking boy: velvet collar and suede shoes; missing are the classic 'Edwardian' drainpipe trousers and string tie.

Teenage boys

There had been little change in men's appearance throughout the forties. In the fifties, a new freedom was apparent, even though for many males standard 'smart' dress was still a suit and tie or sports jacket and grey flannel trousers. Young men slicked down their hair with grease. The traditional 'short back and sides' haircut was still the norm, but it gradually gave way to longer styles with 'quiffs' at the front and short crew-cuts. Fewer young men wore hats, though older men still wore them; if you watch a thirties or forties newsreel, you will see very few men without a cap or hat.

In the USA, Marlon Brando's film *The Wild One* helped popularize a more 'anti-social' fashion — the leather look of the biker or 'greaser'. In Britain, some youths took to wearing 'Edwardian' style clothes; hence the nickname 'teddy boy'. They wore knee-length jackets, narrow 'drainpipe' trousers, bootlace ties, gaudy fluorescent socks and thick crêpe-soled shoes known as 'brothel creepers'. Teddy boys were very particular about their hair which was worn long, greased and swept back, usually with a quiff at the front. The overall effect aimed at a combination of toughness and 'streetwise' smartness. There were sillier, and shorter-lived, fashion crazes: the Walt Disney movie *Davy Crockett* inspired a brief fashion for wearing 'coonskin hats. Pop stars were also influential as fashion-makers. Most of all, boys mimicked Elvis Presley, whose image ranged from tight-jeaned 'macho man' to dandy in gold lamé suit and glittering jewellery.

During the fifties, men moved steadily into the fashion limelight. Another important feature of the decade was that young people in general were becoming self-aware, and

the 'generation gap' was growing. No longer did the young rely on the taste of their elders. They had money in their pockets and a growing range of goods to choose from. They were self-confident, and determined to create their own styles. By so doing, they

Above Fifties clothes were sold as being stylish, hard-wearing and easy to care for. New fabrics with synthetic fibres rapidly replaced traditional woollens and worsteds.

forced designers and manufacturers to follow popular taste rather than try to lead and create it.

Pop Music

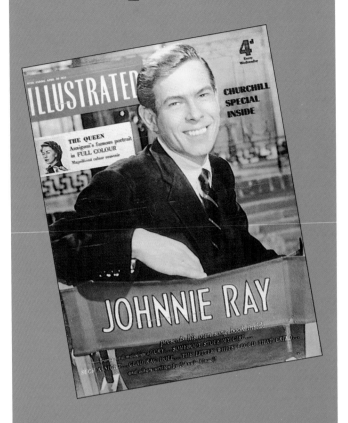

At the start of the fifties, rock music was still in its infancy. Country music, jazz and blues, which were to influence the development of pop, were alive and kicking, but they were 'minority' tastes. Mass-market music was dominated, as it had been throughout the 1930s and 1940s, by the songs from 'Tin Pan Alley', the crooners and the big bands.

The long-playing record had been invented in the USA in 1948, and in 1950 LPs went on sale in Britain. The days of the 78 rpm record were numbered. The 45 rpm single appeared soon after. In 1951 Johnnie Ray had a double-sided million seller with *Cry/Little White Cloud That Cried*. That same year Vera Lynn became the first British artist to top the US charts, with a song called *Auf Wiedersehn Sweetheart*.

Above This cover photo of singer Johnnie Ray, 'Prince of Wails', belies his ability to arouse near-hysteria in fans.

The charts on both sides of the Atlantic were packed with solo singers, male and female. Big names were Jo Stafford, Kay Starr, Doris Day, Guy Mitchell, Frankie Laine, Perry Como and — the megastars of their day — Bing Crosby and Frank Sinatra. For future millionaire stars born in 1950 (who included Peter Gabriel and Stevie Wonder) and 1951 (Sting and Phil Collins), there was not much to rock to in their cradles. However, as these fifties toddlers began to explore the world and their first day at school came nearer, the scene was beginning to change.

The dawn of rock'n'roll

In 1955 Chuck Berry gained an introduction, via blues singer Muddy Waters, to Chess Records in Chicago. His first single was called *Maybelline,* and its arrival in the pop charts heralded the advent of the singer-guitarist, hitherto confined to country music and black music. In that same year, a record by a 28-year-old ex-hillbilly musician named Bill Haley reached number one in the charts all over the world. The event began a musical revolution that seemed, to some critics, likely to threaten the foundations of Western civilization!

The song was *Rock Around the Clock,* which had been featured in the film *Blackboard Jungle.* On its second appearance, it took off and sold by the million. Pop was never to be the same again. Haley and his band, the Comets, were unlikely 'revolutionaries', not exactly in the first bloom of youth. Nonetheless, showings of Haley films caused consternation among the readers of 'respectable' newspapers as they learned of excited teenagers jiving in the aisles – during the screening! Some cinemas banned the Haley films and some US jukebox operators refused to stock rock records. In Connecticut, USA, a theatre lost its licence after a reported riot at a rock show compered by DJ Alan Freed.

Bill Haley, the apparent cause of all this mayhem, must have been as surprised as anyone. His success was short-lived though, and his career declined after three or four years. Into the spotlight which he had momentarily occupied were to step some of the most exciting performers in pop history.

Below Detroit-born Bill Haley moved from hillbilly music to rock'n'roll. Phrases such as 'See You Later Alligator', a 1956 Haley hit, entered the teenage vocabulary. The famous Haley kiss-curl was much copied.

Above Elvis Presley, rock'n'roll's greatest star, was the most photographed celebrity of the fifties. This shot was taken while filming *Love Me Tender* (1956).

Legends of rock

In 1954 a Mississippi-born singer named Elvis Presley had recorded his first single, *That's All Right Mama.* The world remained unmoved, but Presley's switch to the RCA record company in 1956 was the start of the most successful musical career in history. Presley's recording of *Heartbreak Hotel* hit the US charts in April 1956; his appearance on TV's *The Milton Berle Show* attracted a vast nation-wide audience and he was immediately signed up for a film contract.

The rock'n'roll wagon was rolling. Along came a host of performers whose names are now part of pop history; Jerry Lee Lewis, Buddy Holly, the Everly Brothers, Gene Vincent and Little Richard. The fans went wild over these 'new wave' fifties pop stars. Even Johnnie Ray, who was really a middle-of-the-road singer, attracted fervent mobs of fans during his 1956 Australian tour.

On the whole, television programme planners in most countries were slow to react to the popularity of the new stars, and uncertain of how to present them when they did give them air time. Many teenagers tuned in to radio stations in order to hear their favourite music, and the chat from the DJs.

As the second Bill Haley movie *Don't Knock the Rock* did the rounds in 1957, new acts such as the Platters and Frankie Lymon and the Teenagers were drawing wild audiences in the USA. Ricky Nelson made the transition from TV star to teenage idol, and Buddy Holly and the Crickets at last got their big hit with *That'll Be the Day.*

Above Texan Buddy Holly's career began in 1954, singing on local radio. His hallmarks were horn-rimmed glasses and a Fender Stratocaster guitar. In 1958 Holly split with his backing group, the Crickets. He died in 1959.

Above A young amateur skiffle group prepares for a London skiffle competition in 1957. Their instruments are basic: guitars, one-string tea-chest bass, and old-fashioned washboard (right) played with the fingers.

A British phenomenon was skiffle; a 'do-it-yourself' music loosely derived from American country and folk. Youngsters got together to form skiffle groups with such unlikely instruments as washboards and basses made from tea-chests. The leading skiffle star was ex-jazzman Lonnie Donegan whose hits included *Cumberland Gap* and *Puttin' on the Style.* The year was 1957, and in Liverpool John Lennon and Paul McCartney met for the first time, possibly listening to the US number one, Pat Boone's syrupy ballad *Love Letters in the Sand.* They, and thousands of others like them, were picking up guitars and dreaming of stardom.

In 1958 Elvis Presley was drafted for service in the US Army. Fans mourned, but for the Army it was a public relations opportunity not to be missed. Cameras followed the new recruit everywhere as Elvis had his hair cut and abandoned his gold lamé jacket for army uniform. It did not harm his career one bit; his *Jailhouse Rock* was a world-wide hit, and it entered the British charts at number one, the first record ever to do so.

Apart from all this rock excitement, the 1950s saw some other notable musical landmarks. Harry Belafonte's *Mary's Boy Child* was a massive Christmas hit in 1957. Belafonte, a New Yorker, became one of the most respected black entertainers, as singer-songwriter and actor. A 1958 hit was *On the Street Where You Live* by Vic Damone, a song from the Lerner and Loewe smash-hit musical *My Fair Lady.* Harold Jenkins chose one of the least likely stage names — Conway Twitty — and still clocked up a string of hits, from the 1950s to the early 1980s. 1958 saw the solitary single hit, *Donna,* by Richie Valens, a 17-year-old Hispanic American who was to be killed in the 1959 air crash which claimed the lives of DJ-turned-singer The Big Bopper and the great Buddy Holly. Holly's *It Doesn't Matter Anymore* became an immediate hit.

Towards the sixties

The 1950s seemed to end on a downbeat note. Alan Freed was sacked from his radio and TV jobs for refusing to declare that he had never taken 'payola', bribes from record companies. Jazz singer Billie Holiday died in July 1959 as a result of drug and alcohol abuse.

However, there were hopeful signs for the future. Elvis Presley was about to leave the US Army and return to the recording studio after almost two years. In 1959 Berry Gordy Jr founded Motown records, a company which was to play a significant part in the next ten years of pop music. Record players had only just ceased to be wind-up gramophones. Vinyl discs were, as yet, the only medium on which people could buy recorded music; cassettes and CDs were yet to be invented. Most records were mono, although stereo records first went on sale in 1958. There was to be a massive pop music explosion in the decade to come.

The Media

Model CT1381 In Primrose Yellow; also available in Sea Mist Green or White.

During the fifties, almost all areas of the media changed dramatically. Newspapers and magazines became glossier, with larger pictures and more of them, bolder headlines, and more 'sensationalism'. The paperback book increasingly displaced the traditional hardcover edition. The number of radio listeners fell, and so did cinema audiences. Only television went from strength to strength.

Above Advertising had growing power to influence consumer choice. Customers were eager to buy newly available goods, like this refrigerator.

Magazines and newspapers

Few magazines were aimed directly at young people, apart from comics and a few more serious 'up-market' children's magazines such as the British *Eagle* and *Girl.* When readers got too old for *Superman* comics they simply moved on to the daily press. Advertisers were mainly interested in reaching the family at home, rather than the young. Incomes were rising, and though few married women went out to work, women generally were an increasingly attractive target for media advertising. Magazines were full of advertisements for clothes, furniture, cosmetics, children's needs, and domestic appliances.

Teenagers might turn to the readers' letters in these magazines, where 'personal problems' ranging from acne to sex were discreetly discussed. There were no 'frank discussion' radio phone-ins in the 1950s; the letters pages of newspapers and magazines were still almost the only place where people could air subjects that were not talked about in the family. Some subjects — homosexuality, for instance — were not even mentioned in the letters pages.

The fifties was a golden age of sporting heroes — the Harlem Globetrotters basketball team, Mickey Mantle in baseball, tennis players 'Little Mo' Connolly and Lew Hoad, Rocky Marciano the boxer, jockey Gordon Richards, and four-minute miler Roger Bannister among them. The press on the whole treated the stars with great respect, and, unlike today, there were few shocking 'exclusives' exposing the seamier side of professional sport.

Facing page By running the first sub-four-minute mile at Oxford in 1954, medical student Roger Bannister became one of sport's most famous names. Newspapers all over the world carried photos of his record-breaking run.

Sport attracted much media interest, and so too did crime. Murders made news, especially when most convicted murderers faced the death penalty. Show-biz gossip was popular, too. Film stars, rather than pop singers, hit the headlines.

Radio had stolen from the newspapers their claim to be 'first with the news', and television was challenging radio for that position. Newspapers responded by increasing the amount of 'comment'. Regular columnists were as well known as the hosts of today's TV chat shows.

Radio

In Britain there was no commercial radio (nor commercial television) until 1955. Records were seldom heard on BBC radio, other than on request programmes such as *Housewives' Choice* and *Children's Favourites.* The programmes consisted mostly of talks and plays, light music ranging from Latin American bands to organ solos, and variety and comedy half-hours. One wavelength was devoted to 'serious' music and drama.

While in Britain radio remained a monopoly of the British Broadcasting Corporation, in the United States the airwaves were hotly contested by numerous small local commercial stations, operating alongside the major national networks such as CBS and NBC. Small stations were quick to respond to changes in public taste, and eager to satisfy advertising sponsors that they were moving with the times. It was North America that created the DJ, transforming radio from a words-with-music broadcasting medium to a mainly-music format on many stations. As older people switched from radio to TV, programmers saw music-hungry youth as the new radio audience.

The fifties witnessed the end of traditional

Above James Dean in his first film *East of Eden* (1955). Dean's intense, brooding performances made him an idol to young people.

cinema was helping to bring about the breakdown of civilized life. Films with titles such as *Motorcycle Gang* tried to cash in on these concerns, and also draw in a young audience. The young responded enthusiastically to the new acting talents of Marlon Brando and James Dean. Dean in particular, through his two films *East of Eden* and *Rebel Without a Cause,* became a symbol of youthful rebellion. He died tragically at the age of 24, but his reputation is still very much alive.

The 'family film' became less commercially viable, despite the continued success of the Walt Disney studio with 'real-life' nature films, children's classics and animated cartoons. Movie studios turned instead to shock and horror, with a growing output of 'adult only' films. Science fiction movies were

Below Though older than James Dean, Marlon Brando had an equally great appeal to young movie audiences. Films such as *The Wild One* and *On the Waterfront* established his screen persona as rebel.

mass-audience radio entertainment. Popular radio comedians, such as Jack Benny, had been on US radio since the 1930s. However, a new trend was emerging. Radio audiences were falling steadily as more and more people bought television sets. Before long, Jack Benny had moved to TV.

The silver screen
The cinema was at its most popular just after the Second World War. Hollywood glitter, Hollywood stars and Hollywood movies made news world-wide. But during the fifties cinema audiences became smaller and smaller as television took over.

As cinema lost its older audiences, who preferred to stop at home and watch TV quiz shows, Westerns or crime series, it became more reliant on the 'teen-and-twenty' market. This led to the production of more films with a specific 'youth appeal'.

Movie-makers had already begun to examine the problems of young people caught between innocence and experience. During the fifties some adults feared that the

Above A scene from the 1955 science-fiction thriller *This Island Earth*. The theme of humanity threatened by hostile aliens was a fifties favourite with movie-makers. The best of such films are now cult classics.

popular, perhaps because people were worried about the 'progress' of science, especially the atomic bomb, and about the threat of Communism, often symbolically represented in films by terrifying aliens attempting to take over the world. Mad scientists featured in a number of films, usually turning themselves into monsters as a result of their misguided researches. Some of the fifties' science fiction classics, such as *The Incredible Shrinking Man* (1957), *This Island Earth* (1955), *Invasion of the Bodysnatchers* (1956) and *Invaders from Mars* (1953), are still winning fresh audiences today.

By the mid-fifties the Hollywood bubble had burst. Most of the major studios were turning to television, and many cinemas were facing closure as audiences dwindled. By 1957 audience figures were slumping disastrously. There was a real fear that the younger generation would drift away from the cinema entirely — despite the attraction of the cinema theatre and drive-in movie for teenagers seeking privacy on a date.

The cinema turned to technology in an attempt to compete with TV. Various 'wide screen' systems, such as Cinerama and Vistavision, were introduced to woo audiences. Another, less successful, innovation was the 3-D film, for which audiences were issued with special glasses. Despite the undoubted thrill of being able to get a realistic view of the Creature from the Black Lagoon,

Above Poster for the MGM blockbuster *Ben–Hur*, a spectacular big-screen epic made in an attempt to revive dwindling cinema audiences.

3-D films did not win back the vanishing movie audience. Not even such blockbusting epics as *Ben–Hur* (1959) could lure the viewers away from their TV sets.

The small screen

Television created new stars, such as Phil Silvers, who played Sergeant Bilko, and boosted the careers of film actresses such as Lucille Ball, of the long-running *I Love Lucy* series. At the beginning of the fifties, television was still finding its feet, still copying radio and films, unaware of its huge potential. Television, like radio, did not see the young as an important target audience. The first impact of rock'n'roll came from records played on small radio stations and from the film *Rock Around the Clock*. Only after the craze had taken off did television allow the rock stars in front of the camera.

The fifties was the decade in which, for many people, television began to be more 'real' than real life. It had a power that cinema lacked — it brought the everyday world into people's homes.

In 1951 American war hero General Douglas MacArthur made a triumphant tour of the United States. Cities like Chicago staged 'MacArthur Days' to greet him and large crowds jammed the streets. Few spectators in the street could actually see MacArthur, and they grumbled that those who had stayed at home to watch on TV were getting a much better view of what was happening. TV viewers got close-ups from strategically positioned cameras and were

Above One of America's best-loved TV families, as portrayed by Lucille Ball and Desi Arnaz in the long-running *I Love Lucy* show.

Above The coronation of Queen Elizabeth II in Westminster Abbey, 2 June 1953. For the first time, TV cameras broadcast the historic ceremony.

constantly told by the broadcasters that this was a 'great event'. Pictures of waving, cheering crowds were shown. In fact, most of these shots showed people waving to the camera — being on television had become more important than merely seeing a famous person drive by in a car.

Television broadcasters were beginning to see how they could present, and even control, certain events. The coronation of Queen Elizabeth II in 1953, for instance, was televised live, but only after much argument. Traditionalists fiercely opposed the 'intrusion' of the cameras, with their cables and other paraphernalia, into London's Westminster Abbey. Those in favour of televising the ceremony argued, convincingly, that television would add to the occasion by making people throughout Britain and the Commonwealth feel part of the great day. No one since has ever seriously argued against televising such important events.

In the fifties the organization and timing of sports events were still left to the sports bodies, with TV and radio admitted as privileged onlookers and reporters. The televising of major sports such as football, baseball, cricket, tennis, golf and so on did much to increase their popularity. Few people believed that spectators would stay at home and watch their favourite sports on TV. Television could not yet match the thrill of actually being there; the screen was small, the picture black and white (and often shaky), and the camera techniques were very basic.

Advertisers were swift to see the potential of television. TV commercials with their catchy jingles, cartoons, and actors recommending the latest products became as popular as many of the programmes. Politicians were more suspicious, however. During elections, they preferred 'whistle-stop' nation-wide tours and public meetings. When they did agree to appear on television, it was only for carefully controlled and formal 'addresses'. Interviewers were seldom permitted to tackle politicians head-on, and politicians rarely entered into televised debates with their rivals.

All this was to change with the 1960 US election, which saw the famous TV debates between John Kennedy and Richard Nixon. Viewers were allegedly won over by Kennedy's relaxed style and youthful looks which contrasted with the unfortunate Nixon's stubble-darkened complexion and tense manner. After the 1950s no politician could afford to ignore television. And hardly anyone else wanted to.

Leisure

In the fifties the leisure industry was just beginning its remarkable post-war growth. People had more free time as working weeks grew shorter and annual holidays longer. They also had more money to spend. But at first the effects of this social change were slow to appear.

Above The local dance hall on a Saturday night was the favourite meeting place for many fifties couples.

Dancing

Music and dancing were as popular in the fifties as they are today. The usual venue was a large dance hall, and the music was performed 'live' by a dance band, with perhaps a smaller jazz or swing band to fill in. Couples danced together most of the time. The traditional ballroom favourites such as the waltz and quickstep were played. Not everyone knew how to dance them correctly, and dance studios did good business giving lessons to teenagers seeking this essential social skill. The jive, a development of the 1940s jitterbug craze, was the dance which the young adopted as their own, and they danced it to whatever music came along at the right tempo.

Sport and hobbies

Millions of spectators watched live sport. In Britain, soccer drew the largest crowds in its history. In the United States baseball and football were undergoing change: black players regularly featuring in the major

Above The scooter, cheaper than a motorbike, provided low-cost mobility for young people who could not afford the luxury of a car. As in other fields of design, Italian makes (Lambretta and Vespa) were much admired.

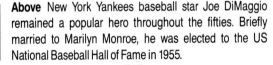

Above New York Yankees baseball star Joe DiMaggio remained a popular hero throughout the fifties. Briefly married to Marilyn Monroe, he was elected to the US National Baseball Hall of Fame in 1955.

leagues, big money franchises increasingly controlling famous-name city teams. TV coverage of the Olympic Games (at Helsinki in 1952 and Melbourne in 1956) did much to increase world-wide sporting interest — even though live satellite transmissions were not yet available.

The sports boom led to professionals in some sports demanding, and receiving, much larger financial rewards. In the USA sports prowess at school offered the prospect of a college scholarship and maybe a lucrative professional career.

While team sports thrived, there was also a growing interest in other pursuits, such as fishing, winter sports, hot-rod racing and surfing. But there were hardly any purpose-built leisure centres or health clubs within the average teenager's price range. The beach and surf lifestyle of California was a million miles away from the streets of the big city. The local tennis or golf club, with its high membership fees, could look almost equally out of reach.

Many teenagers rode bicycles, and some went on to ride motorbikes. Hardly any youngsters outside the USA could afford a car. At home, hobbies were often sexually stereotyped. Boys made models (aircraft were popular). Girls made clothes, sewed and knitted. Collecting things — including stamps, coins and beer-mats — was a passion (often short-lived); so too was writing letters to overseas pen-pals. Teenagers shared their parents' enthusiasm for watching television; it was new.

Below As this 1953 New York Central Railroad advertisement shows, the railways still aimed to attract the long-distance traveller. Competition with airlines intensified with the coming of the jet age, and the railways declined.

Long and Short of Smart Travel
...New York Central style!

Make long jumps on a roomy, restful dieseliner . . . with New York Central to do the driving. Step off fresh, and find a drive-ur-self car ready for short runs at your destination.

Ask your ticket agent to reserve a car for you. Then on your way, instead of grueling hours at the wheel, you can relax in New York Central comfort.

The comfort of conditioned air in a Pullman hotel-room-on-wheels or a streamlined coach with deep, lean-back seats. The comfort of refreshments in the lounge and delicious meals at a dining car table.

Best of all, enjoy the comfort of the Water Level Route . . . through gentle, scenic valleys between East and West.

Make distance just a dream . . . rather than the strain of facing headlights hour after hour. Sleep your way on New York Central . . . yet have a car for your personal use when you arrive.

Travel and holidays

A major difference between the fifties and today is that far fewer people travelled. A foreign holiday was still the preserve of the very rich. Places such as the French Riviera or Venice were just picture postcard names to most people. A survey taken of people in the English town of Derby in 1953 found that only one in four middle-class adults had spent more than two days away from the town in the previous year.

The picture was much the same in other countries. Almost all Americans took their vacations within the USA. Mexico or Canada represented the furthest most ever travelled. Australians went to the beach. Britons, too, went to the seaside, usually by rail or bus. Holiday camps were a popular destination for many; two weeks of 'organized' rest and recreation at a coastal resort, with fun and games provided throughout the day and night, a babysitter for the children in the evening, and everything laid on. Cheap jet travel had not yet made possible the package holiday by air. Apart from those people who travelled abroad as part of their military service (most countries, still had conscription), few had ever set foot on foreign soil.

When people ate in a restaurant, they were unlikely to try foreign food. There were comparatively few 'ethnic' restaurants outside the largest cities, and the fast food chains so familiar today were unheard of outside the USA. For fifties diners there was one innovation: Muzak or 'canned music'. The US Muzak company had begun to develop in the 1930s and by the 1950s had expanded its services so much that background 'music' could be heard not only in restaurants and hotels, but in beauty salons and supermarkets, factories and swimming pools — and even in cemeteries.

MINIMUM CONTENTS
6 FLUID OZS.

Coca-Cola

REG. U.S. PAT. OFF.

Coca-Cola

TRADE MARK

DRINK
Coca-Cola
REG. U.S. PAT. OFF.

Have a Coke

LIFT DOOR
REMOVE BOTTLE

BOTTLE OPENER

COIN RETURN

Drive
Refreshed

Host of the highways

Refresh at the familiar red cooler on the road to anywhere

5¢

Above A 1950 Coca-Cola advertisement featuring a giant automated vending machine. The familiar red drinks dispenser spread from the USA all over the world as American eating and drinking habits became international.

Youth Culture

Teenagers only began to emerge as a distinct group in society during the 1940s. In the 1950s adults first began to express concern, even alarm, at the growth of 'gang culture'. This undesirable phenomenon was blamed on rock'n'roll, and on the relaxation in discipline that had been brought about by the Second World War and its aftermath.

Above The fifties dream: the gleaming chromium-plated car represented glamour and the good life to which many teenagers aspired.

Below The town of Little Rock, Arkansas, became a flashpoint for US civil rights conflict in 1957. The state governor ordered the National Guard to prevent black students from entering segregated whites-only schools.

A disturbing feature was the evidence of racism among youth gangs. In Britain there was a shortage of labour in certain areas — public transport and nursing, for example — and immigration from the Caribbean was encouraged to meet the shortage. Few non-white immigrants had settled in Britain before the fifties. In London and some other cities where the West Indian newcomers settled, they came up against a 'colour bar', particularly when they tried to rent housing. White Teddy boys promoted an outbreak of racial violence in London's Notting Hill district. The 'riot', a minor incident in itself, was a shock to many, and a warning to all.

Racial violence was all too familiar in the United States, where the fifties witnessed an upsurge in blacks' demands for civil rights. The Second World War had caused considerable unrest among black Americans — those suffering unfair working practices at home and those serving in the army. The fifties saw renewed demands for action, and young blacks were prominent in

the campaign — for example, in seeking to register as students in colleges that had previously refused to admit blacks. The Reverend Martin Luther King Jr became leader of the civil rights movement in 1956. A successful boycott of whites-only buses in Montgomery, Alabama, overturned the city's segregation policy. In May 1954 the US Supreme Court ruled that any separation of school pupils because of their race was unconstitutional. But it was to be another decade before Southern states abandoned segregation in schools. Progress towards desegregation was swifter in colleges, and more college-educated blacks entered the world of work demanding the jobs and opportunties for which they were qualified.

Hanging around, having fun

Getting a job was not too difficult for the teenagers of the fifties. But, although this meant that they had money to spend, there

Above A 'Spanish-style' fifties coffee bar. For many young people, the noise of the hissing expresso coffee machine became a familiar accompaniment to juke box music and conversation.

was little entertainment specifically for them. Youth clubs and organizations were popular; four out of ten British teenagers belonged to some kind of club. Coffee bars with juke boxes provided an alternative meeting place. Although many young men proved their manhood by consuming large quantities of beer, to be drunk on the street still carried a social stigma. In many families, it was frowned on for a woman to smoke outside the home. Such behaviour was 'not nice'. The health hazards of cigarette smoking were not widely recognized, and most teenagers quickly followed their elders into the smoking habit. Very few young people took, or even knew about, drugs, which to many were associated with Eastern opium dens, beatniks and the most debauched 'smart' society.

Permissiveness

Despite growing affluence, young people had considerably less freedom in the fifties than they have today. Most lived at home until they got married, went into the armed forces or perhaps went to college. Parents issued 'house rules' and expected that these would be obeyed. How you styled your hair, what you wore, where you went and how late you came home at night: any of these could start an argument. You were not really considered adult until you were 21 and allowed to vote.

The fifties marked the very beginnings of the so-called 'permissive age'. A girl might expect to be kissed on a first date or else she would wonder if there was something wrong with her. She might allow a boy to 'go further' if she liked him enough, and after three or four months dating together she would assume they were 'going steady' and begin to think of getting engaged. Marriage was the goal: to be unmarried was thought 'odd', though two unmarried men could share a home without their neighbours assuming, rightly or wrongly, that they were lovers. To be an unmarried mother was as scandalous as to be homosexual, yet an increasing number of young girls were becoming pregnant. The contraceptive pill had not yet been developed and ignorance in sexual matters was commonplace.

Above The beatniks of the fifties 'dropped out' of conventional society to pursue free-thinking artistic and intellectual life styles. The beatnik movement influenced young people to adopt a more radical, questioning approach to life.

The sexual revolution was only just beginning, and few people would have known what 'sexual stereotyping' meant. Although women were active in many fields, and were working to increase women's opportunities, few girls questioned their role as future wives and mothers. Most were still looking for jobs, not careers, and only a small proportion of female school students went on to higher education. But the numbers were growing, and the women's movement was on its way.

Finding a voice

To many adults 'youth culture' meant 'gangs'. British Teddy boys, with their distinctive dress, seemed a visible symbol of a new and anti-social phenomenon. Hell's Angels racing along US freeways on huge motor-bikes also made good headlines in newspapers, often attracting more outrage than their activities warranted. Teenage crime was on the increase, and the teenage gangs of the 1957 hit musical *West Side Story* had their real-life counterparts. Vandalism in cities was a growing concern, but organized violence (soccer hooliganism, for example) was practically unknown. Most young people were conventional and unquestioning. Organizations such as the Scouts enjoyed a popularity they have not since regained.

Teenagers came together to have fun and share interests. Boys went to clubs to meet girls, and vice versa. Australians and Americans living in the sun belt went to the beach and the barbecue. Blacks and whites tended to socialize separately.

Those belonging to what the media called 'ban the bomb' or 'beatnik' groups met in dimly lit coffee bars — their casual dress, long hair and beards proclaiming their 'protest'. 'Beat' philosophy — pacificism,

Below American teenagers were often portrayed as cheerful, active and involved in harmless pursuits such as this. There are no signs of rebellion or disaffection in this fifties image of youth culture.

mysticism, anarchy, free love, socialism and so on — was to have a great influence on the sixties. Its most famous bard was the American writer and drop-out Jack Kerouac, author of *On the Road* (1957). The fifties beats, a subterranean generation of writers, artists and eccentrics, were the forerunners of the protesters and hippies of the next generation.

Youth was still struggling to find a voice in the fifties. It was not taken seriously by the media, but the seeds of the sixties revolution were being sown. Class barriers were beginning to erode, as young people from different backgrounds mixed more, particularly in the expanding universities and colleges. The post-war 'baby boom' was creating a new generation with fresh hopes.

Fifties Style

To a teenager of today transported back in time, a fifties town would look familiar yet strangely different. The cars were bigger then, more angular, with tailfins, chromium-plated fenders and bulbous headlamps. No one wore safety belts. Steam railway locomotives hissed and puffed in the local station. Most stores gave over-the-counter service; the supermarket was an American innovation of the 1930s and was only just beginning to appear elsewhere.

Above Many shops were still small, like this 1954 example. The owner served customers from behind the counter.

Below The USA had pioneered supermarket shopping in the 1930s. Americans enjoyed growing economic prosperity after the Second World War.

mathematical domes which looked as if they could as easily stand on the surface of Mars as in Missouri. It was also the age of Frank Lloyd Wright's Guggenheim Museum in New York (1959) with its coil-like sweeps and ramps, as well as of Le Corbusier's chapel of Notre-Dame du Haut at Ronchamp (1956). The pace of urban redevelopment had not yet overwhelmed style.

Mies van der Rohe's Seagram Building in New York (1958) is a famous fifties building, a gleaming skyscraper making bold use of dark glass. This vision, of a tall glass tower, was to be endlessly imitated by lesser architects as American cities grew higher, and cities in other countries began to grow for the first time. London's skyline was still dominated by the dome of St Paul's Cathedral, as it had been for almost 300 years, but the gaps made by wartime bombing were to be filled by an undistinguished jumble of concrete and glass. Australia's modern capital, Canberra, was more fortunate. Its development was controlled by the Commission set up by the Australian government in 1958.

Skylines

The 'high-rise' building explosion, too, was just beginning to make its mark on architecture outside the United States. One of the most powerful influences on building style in the fifties was Brutalism, a school of architecture that made little concession to classical ideas of style or beauty. Huge concrete piers held up slab-like tower blocks — topped by an undisguised water tank. Yet the fifties also produced some of the best work of architects such as Buckminster Fuller, the American who became known as the 'Space-Age designer' for his

Above Swiss-born architect Le Corbusier (Charles Edouard Jeanneret, 1887–1965) designed the chapel of Notre-Dame du Haut at Ronchamp in France. It was praised for its daring use of simple lines and shapes.

Design for the home

The fifties saw a new interest in good design, in engineering and in manufacturing generally. The Festival of Britain (1951) and the Brussels World Fair (1958) helped to encourage new ideas. Britain's Festival was a huge success, as people flocked to the different pavilions on the South Bank in London. There were new designs to admire; steel-rod chairs, colourful fabrics, plastic tableware, convertible sofa-beds and domestic appliances. Designers were starting to show what art allied to technology could achieve, and the results were exciting.

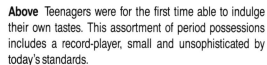

Above Teenagers were for the first time able to indulge their own tastes. This assortment of period possessions includes a record-player, small and unsophisticated by today's standards.

Swedish styling was envied for its simplicity and 'functionalism' — things worked because they were designed to do so. The Scandinavian style used light softwoods in place of the traditional dark hardwoods for furniture and brought a softer, more rounded look to interiors. Magazine advertising played a key role in bringing new designs to people's attention, encouraging them to buy. The kitchen was a main target area — especially in Britain, with so many people being rehoused who had never had the opportunity of owning a 'fitted kitchen'. A greater interest in good design made it possible for even a small kitchen to be replanned on modern lines, with cupboard space, refrigerator, washing machine and so on.

Brighter colours were chosen for walls and ceilings, replacing the browns and greens commonplace in the pre-war period. Everything was 'contemporary' — a word over-used by advertisers. Contrasting designs of wallpaper, curtains, carpets and furnishings were encouraged.

Style on the road

The ambition of almost every family was to have a TV and a car. Cars in particular were advertised constantly as the 'dream purchase', with the family car pictured being cleaned, petted, and shown off before admiring neighbours. Few people in the USA or Britain owned, or even saw, a foreign-built car and in the early fifties many drivers were happy to buy a pre-war design. However, new models appeared every year; crowds flocked

Above This 1952 US advertisement describes the 'dream kitchen', which offers 'beauty and unheard-of work savings'. Images such as this fuelled people's desire for better, more modern, homes.

Above This 1950 Cadillac was basically the same as pre-war designs. It was roomy, heavy on fuel, and resplendent with chrome. Americans were still enjoying cheap gasoline, and 'gas-guzzling' was not yet a problem.

to motor shows and salerooms. While American cars became bigger and shinier, European cars got more compact. A style breakthrough was Alec Issigonis's Mini (1959), a tiny front-engined car which was destined to be one of the symbols of the sixties. Less successful was the Ford Edsel (1958), the greatest financial flop in US auto industry history because no one liked its huge grilles.

Modernism

The fifties brought a new awareness of design. Wartime austerity and utility were replaced by styles which combined new materials with a look deliberately adopted for its 'modernism'. Abstract art moved into the commercial world, and design schools began to work much more closely with industry. Good design sells products; that was the message being spread.

Certain phrases current in the fifties are still with us: 'gift department', 'leisure clothing', 'best-seller' — and, above all, 'image' — public image, brand image, corporate image. Designers were more and more aware of the importance of creating an image that would win 'customer loyalty'. Modernism demanded new, snappy names; it was by design that the International Business Machines Corporation became simply IBM. It was a sign of the times.

Images of the Fifties

The shadow of the bomb

The USA was the world's only nuclear power until 1950, when Russia claimed to have its own atomic bomb. In October 1952 Britain tested an A-bomb and a month later the USA exploded the world's first hydrogen bomb at Eniwetok Atoll in the Pacific. The new weapon was far more powerful than the atomic bombs dropped on Japan in 1945, and its mushroom cloud sent a wave of apprehension around the world.

The Russians were quick to counter with an H-bomb of their own. The two super-powers now had weapons terrible enough to destroy not only each other, but the entire planet. 'Mutual assured destruction' became the philosophy behind the nuclear deterrent.

Above The mushroom cloud of the first H-bomb test in 1952 ushered in a new era of armed insecurity.

Boeing wins the jet race

Boeing's four-engined 707 airliner first flew in July 1954. It was not the first jet transport to enter service. Britain's Comet had made its maiden flight in 1949 and began carrying passengers in May 1952. But a series of accidents in 1954 caused the Comet to be temporarily withdrawn, and it was Boeing that picked up the commercial prizes. More than 900 707s were built, and many are still flying today.

The 707's capacity (167 passengers), range (it could fly non-stop from New York to London), and speed (cruising at 978 km/hr) brought in a new age of air travel. It halved the flight time across the Atlantic, and its success signalled the end for both piston-engined airliners and transatlantic ocean liners such as the *Queen Elizabeth* and *United States*.

Below Boeing's four-jet 707 airliner profited from the misfortunes of its rival, De Havilland's Comet. With jet travel, cheap long-haul holidays became a reality.

Raising the independence flag

Britain's once-vast Empire was shrinking. On 6 March 1957 the Gold Coast, in West Africa, became the first British colony in Africa to achieve independence. The British flag was lowered and the flag of the new nation, renamed Ghana, was raised in its place. Ghana's first president was Kwame Nkrumah, who was to be prominent among a new generation of Third World leaders. Britain's prime minister, Harold Macmillan, spoke of a 'wind of change' in Africa. In fact, the world map was being redrawn, as the territories of the old Empire gained their independence during the late fifties and, especially, the early sixties. Most remained within the Commonwealth — no longer a 'white club', but a free association of diverse nations and peoples.

Facing page Ghana's new leader, Dr Kwame Nkrumah, salutes cheering crowds at midnight on 6 March 1957 – independence day.

Dawn of the space age

On 4 October 1957 the world heard a faint, but momentous, sound: the 'bleep bleep' signal of the world's first artificial satellite. Sputnik I, a spherical device 58 cm in diameter and weighing just under 84 kilograms, was blasted into orbit around the Earth by a Soviet rocket.

The Russians' achievement startled Western scientists, some of whom had openly scoffed at the suggestion that spaceflight was yet possible. As Sputnik I circled the Earth, its radio signals heralding the new space age, American space scientists scrambled to launch their own satellite. The 'space race' was about to begin.

Above The world's first space satellite, Sputnik 1, was a small globe bearing long radio antennae. It could do little but reveal its presence by a monotonous signal. Yet its launch marked a major advance in human progress.

Below Cuba's new Marxist leader, Fidel Castro, in 1959. Castro's battledress, beard and pistol symbolized revolution. The world waited to see how he would change Cuba.

Revolution in America's backyard

The island of Cuba, long a haven for rich tourists, gamblers and the underworld, was in the news throughout 1959. The corrupt dictatorship of Fulgencio Batista was overthrown by a Marxist revolution, led by a lawyer named Fidel Castro. The 32-year-old Castro became the ultimate Communist bogeyman for Americans, who viewed with alarm the prospect of a Communist state, armed and supplied by Russia, so close to the American mainland. The US government feared that Cuban-style revolution might occur throughout Central and South America. Castro's lieutenant, Che Guevara, was to become a sixties revolutionary hero, while Castro himself has remained Cuba's leader for three decades.

Nuclear power

The fifties saw the beginning of civil nuclear power. A Soviet station at Obninsk, near Moscow, was reported operational in June 1954, but the first large-scale nuclear generating plant was Britain's Calder Hall, opened in Cumbria on 17 October 1956. The promise of infinite supplies of cheap electricity was a tempting one for a world

Above The British nuclear power station at Calder Hall. Nuclear power was greeted enthusiastically: a fire here in 1957 passed relatively unnoticed.

recovering from the ravages of war. Calder Hall, and the other stations that followed, were greeted with enthusiasm. Few people foresaw the environmental hazards of nuclear waste. For most, Calder Hall seemed to herald a technological golden age.

Above Edmund Hillary's photo shows Tenzing Norgay on the summit of Everest. To many, this mountaineering triumph seemed to herald a new age of achievement.

Everest conquered

As Britain prepared to celebrate Coronation Day, 2 June 1953, there came dramatic news of a long-awaited triumph. Mount Everest, the world's highest mountain, had finally been climbed, after seven unsuccessful attempts. Two mountaineers — a New Zealander, Edmund Hillary, and a Nepalese Sherpa, Tenzing Norgay — had done what so many brave climbers had tried and failed to accomplish. They were members of a Commonwealth expedition led by Colonel John Hunt. Hillary and Tenzing climbed up the final snow ridge to the summit at 9 am on 29 May. When they returned to their base camp, the news was flashed by radio around the world, most of Britain hearing it on Coronation Day itself.

The Suez crisis

The Suez Canal is a vital international waterway, linking the Red Sea with the Mediterranean. In 1956 Egypt's President Nasser threatened to nationalize it (the Canal had been run since 1875 by a British-controlled company). Britain and France, acting secretly with Israel, staged a brief and disastrously unsuccessful invasion of the Canal zone. When the USA refused to back their action, they were forced to withdraw. Egypt took over the running of the Canal and the sorry affair led to the eventual resignation of Britain's prime minister, Anthony Eden.

Above A British reconnaissance photo shows bombed fuel tanks burning near the Suez Canal during the military adventure of 1956, which ended in humiliation.

Marching for equality

For many years minority groups in the USA (blacks, Indians, Hispanics and others) had suffered from discrimination. Education was a key issue in the fifties. In 1954 the US Supreme Court declared that segregation of blacks and whites into separate schools must end. Discrimination in housing and jobs was also condemned. But court rulings did not bring about instant equality. Blacks took to the streets to demand civil rights for all.

Above Civil rights marchers in the USA. The movement startled its opponents by its ability to mobilize blacks of all ages in a common cause. Thousands marched, with songs and placards, to back their political demands.

From 1956 the civil rights movement had a new and inspiring leader in the Reverend Martin Luther King Jr. He led the struggle into the Southern states of the USA, heartland of prejudice, as the movement gathered momentum for the massive campaigns and victories of the sixties.

 Above Defiance in Budapest, as Hungarians burn a Soviet flag to show their resistance shortly before Soviet forces invaded and quelled the uprising.

The Hungarian uprising

Since the end of the Second World War Hungary, like other Eastern European states, had been in the iron grip of Soviet rule. Its Communist government was deeply unpopular and in October 1956 huge crowds flocked on to the streets of the Hungarian capital Budapest, demanding reforms and the removal of all Soviet troops.

At first it seemed the Hungarians might win their freedom, but in November Budapest was stormed by Russian tanks. The revolt was brutally crushed, and thousands of Hungarians fled the country as refugees. A Soviet 'puppet', Janos Kadar, was installed to head the Hungarian government, while ex-premier and moderate Imre Nagy was seized and later executed for 'treason'.

An end to the polio scare

In the early fifties many young people lived in fear of an epidemic of polio. Polio (poliomyelitis) is a virus infection which affects the brain and nervous system.

Outbreaks were worst in warm weather, and victims were often left paralyzed. Children were warned to avoid swimming pools and over-exertion in sports during epidemics (which occurred in several years following the Second World War).

In 1955 the first American children were given an anti-polio vaccine developed by Dr Jonas Salk. A British vaccine similar to Salk's was first used in 1956 and from 1958 an oral vaccine was available. Immunization was a great success, ending the fear of the hot-summer polio epidemic — though it is still important for children to be vaccinated against the disease.

 Above Dr Jonas Salk, whose polio vaccine saved many lives. His own sons were among the first to be given experimental injections.

War in Korea

The Korean War of 1950 to 1953 was the major fifties flashpoint between East and West. In 1945 Korea (occupied by Japan during the Second World War) had been divided. The North had a Communist government under Soviet influence. The South was non-Communist and backed by the USA.

In 1950 Communist troops from North Korea invaded the South, and the 'cold war' between the superpowers was fanned into flame. United Nations forces, mostly Americans but with troops from fifteen other

 Above A US mortar in action during the Korean War. About 480,000 Americans fought in Korea, of whom some 157,000 were either killed or wounded.

UN members including Britain, Canada and Australia, were sent to repel the invasion. Communist China sent a 'volunteer army' to aid the North Koreans and US Sabre aircraft clashed with Russian-built Chinese MiGs in the first-ever jet dogfights. The war ground on, with neither side able to force a victory, until 1953. The Panmunjon treaty brought a truce, but no peace settlement; the two Koreas have remained mutually hostile ever since.

Glossary

Affluence   An abundant supply of money, property or wealth.

Allies   Nations united in alliance to fight Germany and Japan during the Second World War.

Anarchy   Disorder or chaos resulting from the absence or failure of government. Anarchists believe in a totally free society, without government.

Austerity   When consumer goods and luxuries are in short supply.

British Empire   Territories ruled by Britain. By the fifties the British Empire, which in the nineteenth century covered a quarter of the world, was shrinking as colonies became independent.

Civil rights movement   The campaign by blacks in the USA to win full equality under the US Constitution.

Cold War   The period of antagonism between the Communist East, led by the USSR, and the capitalist West, the USA and its allies. It reached its height during the early 1950s.

Commonwealth   Association of states formerly within the British Empire.

Communism   A political theory aiming to establish a society where the major enterprises such as factories, mines, farms and shops are owned by all citizens rather than a class of wealthy people. In practice, Communist societies have tended to create powerful state authorities which control those enterprises.

Conscription (or **draft**)   Compulsory enlistment in the armed forces.

Contraceptive   A device used to prevent unwanted pregnancy.

Coronation   The crowning of a monarch. Queen Elizabeth II was crowned on 2 June 1953.

Epidemic   A word to describe a disease affecting a lot of people at the same time.

European Economic Community (EEC)   An association of Western European countries, brought into being by the Treaty of Rome (1957) signed by France, West Germany, Italy, Belgium, Luxembourg and the Netherlands. The United Kingdom, the Irish Republic and Denmark joined in 1973, and Spain, Portugal and Greece are also now members.

Four-minute mile   A long-sought-after record in track running. Roger Bannister became the first person to run a mile in under four minutes in May 1954.

Franchise   In US sport, a baseball or football franchise is a team which can be bought and sold, like a business. In 1953, for example, the Boston Braves baseball team moved to Milwaukee.

Haute couture   French for 'high fashion'.

Hell's Angels   Groups identified with high-powered customized motorbikes, and sometimes associated with gang violence.

Holiday camp   A type of holiday centre popular in the UK during the fifties. Guests stayed in cabins or chalets, and food and entertainment were provided for them.

Homosexual   Someone sexually attracted to members of the same sex; particularly a man who is attracted to other men. Women attracted to other women are more usually called lesbians.

Immunization   Protecting people from a disease, usually through an injection.

Mysticism   Philosophical and religious belief in the possibility of making direct contact with God.

Nationalize   To put an industry under the control of the state.

Nuclear deterrent   Atomic weapons;

deterrence strategy holds that if opposing sides have equally strong nuclear forces, neither will ever use such weapons.

Pacifism The belief that all forms of violence are wrong, and that people should not fight in wars.

Payola Bribes paid to persuade a DJ to play certain records.

Permissiveness A view of life which holds that people should be allowed to do as they please, with as little interference as possible.

Pop art A form of art glorifying the modern, mass-produced images of comics, TV and advertising.

Rationing Restricting the distribution of goods which are in short supply. In Britain many things were rationed during the Second World War, and rationing did not end completely until 1954.

Segregation The separation of people according to race, as practised in some US states during the fifties, and in South Africa to this day.

Sexual stereotyping The assumption that men and women have certain fixed roles in society; for example, that men go out to work while women stay at home as housewives and mothers.

Synthetic Something made artificially.

Tin Pan Alley A district in a city associated with the production of popular music. Originally it referred to an area of New York. It is mainly used to describe 'commercial' popular music prior to rock'n'roll.

Further Reading

Pop from the Beginning, Nik Cohn (Weidenfeld and Nicolson, 1969)

Fashion in the Forties and Fifties, Jane Dorner (Ian Allan, 1975)

The Forties and Fifties, Nathaniel Harris (Macdonald, 1975)

Life in Britain in the Fifties, Sarah Harris (Batsford, 1985)

Growing Up in the 1950s, C.A.R. Hills (Batsford, 1983)

A Family in the Fifties, Alison Hurst (A. & C. Black, 1987)

The Fifties, Peter Lewis (Ian Allan, 1975)

Growing Up in the Fifties, Jeremy Pascall (Wayland, 1980)

General background

A Short History of the Post-War World, 1945-1970, Duncan Taylor (Dobson, 1977)

The Age of Upheaval: the World Since 1914, J.M. Roberts (Penguin, 1981)

Picture Acknowledgements

Barnaby's Picture Library 8t, 31, 38; Camera Press 44t, 44b; Kobal Collection 14t, 20t, 20b, 21, 22t; Novosti 40b; Peter Newark 6b, 7, 11, 26, 27, 35t; Photri 35b, 37, 43; Popperfoto front cover, 5, 9t, 10, 16, 24, 25t, 25b, 29t, 33t, 45; TOPHAM 4, 6t, 8b, 9b, 12, 13, 14b, 15, 17, 18, 22b, 23, 28, 29b, 30, 32, 33b, 34, 36, 39, 40t, 41, 42t, 42b.

Index